Andy Pa

jack-in-t

Story by Maria Bird

Illustrated by Matvyn Wright

HODDER & STOUGHTON

One day when Teddy came to play with Andy Pandy, he found him looking at a big box. 'What is it?' asked Teddy. 'I don't know,' Andy said. 'The postman brought it.'

He felt all round it, and he knocked on it, and he tried to lift the lid. Then Teddy felt all round it, and *he* knocked on it, and *he* tried to lift the lid.

No good. The box wouldn't open. They were quite tired, so they climbed on top of the box and sat on it to think. Suddenly it flew open with a bang and shot them off.

When they came down to the floor there was a merry face smiling at them. A black face with fuzzy hair and red eyes. 'It's a Jack-in-the-box,' said Andy Pandy, rubbing his elbows.

'Has he come to play with us?' asked Teddy. But before Andy could answer —BANG went the lid, and the Jack-in-the-box had gone. 'Next time,' Teddy said, 'I'll put my paws in, then he can't shut the lid.'

So they waited. And sure enough the lid opened a little way and the merry black face peeped out. Quick as lightning Teddy put his paws in. Before you could say 'Jack-in-the-box'—

He had pulled Teddy in with him, and all Andy Pandy could see was a bit of yellow fur which wouldn't go in. 'Well,' said Andy, 'I'll have to be quicker next time.' Then he hid behind the box.

Soon Jack peeped out again. So did Teddy. But when they couldn't see Andy Pandy they pushed the lid farther back. As soon as it was far enough, Andy Pandy caught it and pulled it wide open.

'It's very nice in here,' Teddy said. 'You come in too, Andy Pandy.' 'I'm much too big,' said Andy Pandy, but Jack and Teddy each took one of Andy's hands and pulled him in. Then bang went the lid again.

To Andy's surprise they fitted in quite nicely. He and Teddy and Jack all seemed to be about the same size, and there they were in a little room with tables and chairs and a nice warm carpet on the floor.

There were plates and cups, and in the corner was a little bed with BLACK SHEETS to match Jack's smiling face. There was even a wash basin with a real tap, and the water was as black as ink. Teddy washed in it to see.

Jack gave them some biscuits and they enjoyed themselves very much. Then Andy Pandy said, 'Thank you for having us, but I think we must go home now.'

'Nothing easier,' said Jack.

BISCUIT

Suddenly Andy Pandy found himself curled up on his own floor. Teddy was asleep beside him, and between them was a Jack-in-the-box. Not a big one, but an ordinary little one. 'Well,' said Andy, 'I must have been dreaming!'

Andy Pandy told Teddy all about it, and Teddy liked the idea of washing in ink so much that he fetched a bottle and poured it over himself. It took Andy half an hour to make him clean again.

'Oh dear,' said Teddy while he was being dried, 'I wish it hadn't been only a dream.' 'It was a nice dream,' said Andy. 'Yes,' said Teddy, 'but I would like to have seen Jack's house and his bed, and his little black face on his little black pillow.'

A SELECTION OF ANDY PANDY BOOKS

Andy Pandy and the willow tree
Andy Pandy and the white kitten
Andy Pandy and the gingerbread man
Andy Pandy in the country
Andy Pandy's shop
Andy Pandy's jack-in-the-box
Andy Pandy and the snowman
Andy Pandy's weather house
Andy Pandy's new pet
Andy Pandy's red motor car

Printed in Great Britain for
Hodder & Stoughton Children's Books,
Salisbury Road, Leicester
by Adams Brothers & Shardlow Ltd, Leicester

15 16 17 18